The Grate-est Joke Book Ever!

The Very Best Puns, Pickup Lines, Wordplay, and Cheesy Humor For Adults!

By: Rilee Ann

The Grate-est Joke Book Ever! - The Very Best Puns, Pickup Lines, Wordplay, and Cheesy Humor For Adults!

ISBN-13:978-1974434428
ISBN-10:1974434427

The Grate-est Joke Book Ever! - The Very Best Puns, Pickup Lines, Wordplay, and Cheesy Humor For Adults!

Table of Contents

A Blurb About Me and This Book

I enjoy jokes. That's right. JOKES. Jokes of any kind, including those stupid ones with no punch line that make no sense and nothing funny is actually said and it's so bad it makes everyone around you face palm hard enough to leave hand prints.

I find humor in everything and by everything, I mean **everything,** and can find something funny in any situation. It's probably not the best way to deal with problems and I will eventually make plenty of enemies due to my inconsiderate, poorly timed comments. My overall lack of a filter won't help either, but it's fine and I enjoy it so, screw them.

There really isn't any form of humor that I don't like. Puns, pickup lines, stories, movies, knock-knock jokes, even the ones that your old chemistry teacher pulls from his collection of "helpful" jokes. You know, the one he thought was just absolutely wonderful and used in an effort to give that boring lecture about isotopes or photosynthesis (the lectures you never really paid attention to anyway) a bit of humor? I love those.

I guess people tend to call my "obsession" with humor "unhealthy" but that just seems a little exaggerated. I've spent years collecting things that I found funny, witty, and/or clever, writing them down and saving hundreds of punny images (I still don't see where the "unhealthy obsession" idea came into play) with no intention of sharing any of them. That's right, I did it just for fun. However, plans changed, and now the best jokes I have ever seen or heard are neatly compiled here in this book for you to enjoy. This is a privilege. I'm doing you a favor. Consider yourself lucky.

I like to laugh and I like to make other people laugh, so I've put this book together to make you pee yourself with laughter. Or at the very least produce a few chuckles. Need some humor in your life? You got it. Don't need any humor in your life? Too bad.

My goal here isn't to offend anyone on purpose, so don't take these too personally. If you're offended, that's a shame, I've done my job, get over it or put the book down. Besides, you've probably got a crappy sense of humor anyway.

There is no shortage of jokes in the world and I thoroughly enjoyed the time I spent discovering all the ones that I'm about to share with you.

Have fun!

Questions

What is a joke? What is funny? What is the point of laughter if we're all just going to die anyway? Why did my questions get so dark so fast? Why am I sad now? What's the point? Here you find the answers to life's toughest and deepest questions.

- Can February March? No but April May.
- Where do you drown a hipster? In the mainstream.
- How do hipsters talk about shoes? They converse.
- What did the buffalo say when his son left for college? Bison.
- What do you call someone with no body and no nose? Nobody nose.
- What happened when a ship carrying red paint, collided with a ship carrying blue paint? Both crews were marooned.
- What does a grape say when it gets stepped on? Nothing. It just lets out a little wine.
- What does a clock do when it's hungry? It goes back four seconds.
- Why did the scarecrow win an award? He was outstanding in his field.
- What concert costs 45 cents? 50 cent and Nickelback.
- What's great about living in Switzerland? Well, the flag is a big plus.
- Why is it a bad idea to hunt bald eagles? Because it's ill-eagle.
- What kind of bees make milk? Boo-bees.
- Why are there no knock-knock jokes about America? Because freedom rings.

- Why are fish so easy to weigh? Because they come with their own scales.
- What did the pirate say when he turned 80? Aye Matey.
- How do you think the unthinkable? With an itheberg.
- Why does a chicken coop have two doors? If it had four doors, it would be a chicken sedan.
- What do you call a sleeping dinosaur? A dinosnore.
- Why was the cook arrested? For possession of pots.
- How did the intruder get in? In-tru-da window.
- Where did Noah keep his bee's? In the ark-hives.
- What do you call a dinosaur with an extensive vocabulary? A thesaurus.
- What kind of shoes does a thief wear? Sneakers.
- What kind of shoes do plumbers hate? Clogs.
- How many optometrists does it take to change a lightbulb? 1 or 2? 1...or 2?
- How does Moses make his tea? Hebrews it.
- Why were the Indians here first? They had reservations.
- How do astronauts say they are sorry? They Apollo-gize.
- What did the duck say when she bought lipstick? Put it on my bill.
- What do sea monsters eat for lunch? Fish and ships.
- Which day do chickens hate the most? Fry-day.
- Why didn't the skeleton go to prom? Because he had no body to dance with.
- How do you make Holy water? Burn the hell out of it.

- 1 joke in 5 different languages:

  English: Where do cats go when they die? PURRgatory.

  Spanish: ¿De dónde van los gatos cuando mueren? PurGATOrio.

  Italian: Dove vanno i gatti quando muoiono? Nel purGATTOrio.

  French: Où vont les chats quand ils meurent? Au purCHATtoire.

  Portuguese: Para onde os gatos vão quando morrem? Para o purGATOrio.

- What happens to a frog's car when it breaks down? It gets toad.

- How do you kill a vegan vampire? With a steak to the heart.

- What do you call someone who doesn't fart in public? A private tutor.

- Why do seals swim in salt water? Because pepper water makes them sneeze.

- Where do astronauts hang out? At the space bar.

- What's worse than raining cats and dogs? Hailing taxi cabs.

- Why can't you play hide-and-seek with mountains? They are always peaking.

- Did you hear the story about the giraffe? Forget it, it's too long.

- How do hippies like their potatoes? Hashed.

- What does a cannibal call someone in a really good mood? A happy meal.

- Why didn't the lifeguard save the hippy? He was too far out.

- What is a pirate's favorite letter? You make think it's 'r' but his first love be the 'c'.

- Where do golf balls hang out? At the club.

- Want to know how I got out of Iraq? Iran.

- Why did the hipster burn his tongue? He drank his coffee before it was cool.

- What did one strawberry say to the other? If you weren't so fresh, we wouldn't be in this jam.

- Why can't a bicycle stand on its own? Because it's two-tired.

- Do you want to hear a joke about paper? Never mind. It's tearable.

- What do pirates and trumpet players have in common? They both murder on the high C's.

- Why did the picture go to jail? Because it was framed.

- Why did they fire the cross-eyed teacher? Because he couldn't control his pupils.

- What do you get when you mix alcohol and literature? Tequila Mockingbird.

- What do you call an alligator in a vest? An investigator.

- What do you call a guy with no arms and no legs at your door? Matt.

- Did you hear about the english teacher who went to jail? She got a full sentence.

- Why do cows have hooves instead of feet? Because they lactose.

- What do you call a psychic midget who has escaped from prison? A small medium at large.

- What does a nosy pepper do? Get jalapeño business.

- How did the farmer find his wife? He tractor down.

- How is imitation like a plateau? They are both the highest forms of flattery.

- What's the difference between a guitar and a fish? You can tune a guitar but you can't tuna fish.

- Did you hear about the constipated mathematician? He worked his problem out with a pencil. It was a No. 2 pencil.

- What kind of bagel can fly? A plain bagel.

- How many South Americans does it take to change a lightbulb? A Brazilian.

- How do the trees feel in the spring? Re-leaved.

- What do you call bears with no ears? B.

- Why is it named the English Channel instead of the BB Sea?

- What do you call a laughing piano? A Yamahahaha.

- What tea do hockey players drink? Penaltea.

- What's the difference between a poorly dressed man on a bicycle and a nicely dressed man on a tricycle? A tire.

- Why are graveyards so noisy? Because of all the coffin.

- How much room is needed for fungi to grow? As mushroom as possible.

- Why did the cows return to the marijuana field? It was the pot calling the cattle back.

- What do you call a group of babies? An infantry.

- Change is hard. Have you ever tried to bend a coin?

- What do you call a dictionary on drugs? High-definition.

- What do you call an everyday potato? A commentator.

- What do you call a cow with no legs? Ground beef.

- Why did the banana go to the doctor? It wasn't peeling well.

- What do you call an owl that does magic tricks? Hoodini.

- What do you call a group of singing dinosaurs? A tyrannochorus.

- What do you call a thieving alligator? A crookodile.

- What do Russians call it when they don't have internet connection? Interniet.

- Why do people litter? Because they don't take the "please don't litter" signs litterally.

- What kind of shorts do clouds wear? Thunderwear.

- How does the man on the moon cut his hair? Eclipse it.

- Which American president was the least guilty? Lincoln. He was in-a-cent.

- What kind of exercise do lazy people do? Diddly-squats.

- Where do animals go when their tails fall off? The retail store.

- Why can't you hear a pterodactyl go to the bathroom? Because the 'P' is silent.

- I met a girl with 12 nipples. Sounds crazy, dozen tit?

- What do you call a broken can opener? A can't opener.

- Why does Trump take anti-anxiety medication? To prevent hispanic attacks.

- What was the barista's favorite part about being arrested? The mug shots.

- Why did the blind man fall into the well? Because he couldn't see that well.

- How do you count cows? With a cowculator.

- What do llamas ride in to go to prom? A llamaousine.

- What do you call dental X-rays? Tooth pics.

- What do you call a guy with no arms and no legs in the water? Bob.

- Did you hear about the time I dipped a strawberry in chocolate? I really had fonduing it.

- Are people that manufacture tabletops counterproductive?

- Want to hear a word I just made up? Plagiarism.

- How do Japanese Chihuahuas say hello? "Konichihuahua".

- How do you organize a space party? You planet.

- When's the best time to go to the dentist? Tooth-hurty.

- What does a house wear? Address.

- Why aren't koalas actual bears? They don't meet the koalifications.

- What did the left eye say to the right eye? "Between you and me, something smells."

- Why did the cowboy get a wiener dog? He wanted to get a long little doggie.

- Why was 6 afraid of 7? Because 7 was a registered 6 offender.

- What do you call a big pile of kittens? A meowntain.

- Do you want to hear a pizza joke? Never mind, it's pretty cheesy.

- Did you see the movie about the hot dog? It was an Oscar Wiener.

- Did you hear about the crime that happened in a parking garage? It was wrong on so many levels.

- Did you hear about the fire at the shoe factory? Real tragedy. 100 soles were lost.

- Which idiot called him Alexander Graham Bell and not Lord of the Rings?

- When is a door not a door? When it's ajar.

- Need an ark to save two of every animal? I Noah guy.

- What do ghosts serve for dessert? I scream.

- Did you hear the joke about the high wall? It's hilarious. I'm still trying to get over it.

- Did you hear about the kidnapping at the school? It's fine now, he woke up.

- If two meth addicts start dating, is it called speed dating?

- What if soy milk is just regular milk introducing itself in Spanish?

- How do you get a baby alien to sleep? You rocket.

- Does running late count as exercise?

- What do you call a cow with a twitch? Beef jerky.

- Did you know that bee keepers have famously attractive eyes? I don't know the science behind it but studies show beauty is in the eye of the bee-holder.

- Did you hear about these new reversible jackets? I'm excited to see how they turn out.

- Did you hear about the two guys who stole a calendar? They each got six months.

- What do you call a bird at a party? A party foul.

- If Apple made a car, would it have windows?

- If I refuse to take a nap, is that resisting a rest?

- This guy said to me, "I'm going to smack you with the neck of this guitar." So I said to him, " Is that a fret?"

- So I was in the store and saw a man throwing milk and cheese about. I looked at him and thought, "How dairy?"

- Do you think prison guards use proactive to prevent breakouts?

- If a plant is sad, do other plants photo-sympathize with it?

- What idiot called it 'possession of marijuana' and not 'joint custody'?

- What do you get when you cross a snowman with a vampire? Frostbite.

- What do you call a pig that does karate? Pork chop.

- What do you call a lazy kangaroo? A pouch potato.

- What do you call an academically successful slice of bread? An honor roll.

- Did you hear about the Italian chef with a terminal illness? He pastaway.

- What do prisoners use to call each other? Cell phones.

- What did the ocean say to the beach? Nothing, it just waved.

- Why did the bee get married? Because he found his honey.

- What's the difference between a politician and a flying pig? The letter F.

- Why don't cannibals eat clowns? They taste funny.

- What do you call a frog stuck in mud? Unhoppy.

- Why can't pigs tell a joke? Because they're such a bore.

- What do vampires take when they are sick? Coffin drops

- What do magicians and hockey players have in common? Both do hat tricks.

- Did you hear about the monkey with a steak on his head? He thought he was a grill-a.

- Why don't some couples go to the gym? Because some relationships don't work out .

- Why don't programmers like nature? It has too many bugs.

- Did you know they won't be making yard sticks any longer?

- What do you call a bald monster? A lock-less monster.

- If you lose your hearing, is it ear replaceable?

- What's a mummy's favorite type of music? Wrap.

- What do dogs do after they finish obedience school? They get their masters.

- Why did the pig stop sunbathing? He was bacon in the heat.

- What did the man say when the bridge fell on him? "The suspension is killing me."

- Pencils could be made with erasers on both ends, but what would be the point?

- What is a thesaurus' favorite dessert? Synonym buns.

- Where do you imprison a skeleton? In a rib cage.

- What kind of rooms have no walls? Mushrooms.

- Did you hear about the restaurant on the moon? The food is great but there is no atmosphere.

- What do vegetarian zombies eat? Graaaaains.

- What did the blanket say as it fell off the bed? Oh sheet.

- What can jump higher than a house? Anything. Houses can't jump.

- Why do cows have bells? Because their horns don't work.

- Why did the football coach go to the bank? To get his quarterback.

- What do you get when you cross an elephant and a fish? Swimming trunks.

- What kind of storm is always in a rush? A hurry-cane.

- Which ghost is the best dancer? The boogie man.

- What's a scarecrow's favorite fruit? Straw-berries.

- Why didn't the police catch the banana? Because it split.

- What type of bee can't make up its mind? A maybe.

- What did the fish say when he ran into the wall? Dam.

One Liners

Have you ever noticed how the coolest people speak in single sentences? Take Arnold Schwarzenegger for example. "I'll be back", "Get to the choppa". He practically only speaks with single sentences and he's freaking awesome. He's a total badass. Now it's your turn. Here are some of the best one liners ever. I guarantee you'll be just as cool as Arnold if you constantly use these in every day conversation. Maybe even cooler. Do you know why? These aren't just one liners. They're puns too. BAM.

◆ Orcas can do some killer whale impressions.

◆ Well, to be Frank, I'd have to change my name.

◆ I've just written a song about tortillas... actually, it's more of a rap.

◆ I, for one, like Roman numerals.

◆ Two fish are in a tank, then one turns to the other and asks, "How do you drive this thing?"

◆ A dung beetle walks into a bar and asks, "Is this stool taken?"

◆ I bought shoes off a drug dealer; I don't know what he laced them with but I've been tripping all day.

◆ Whiteboards are remarkable.

◆ I burned my Hawaiian pizza today; I should have cooked it at aloha temperature.

◆ Skeletons can't lie because you can see right through them.

◆ I'm so bright my mother calls me son.

◆ When I found out my toaster wasn't waterproof, I was shocked.

◆ I gave my dead batteries away, free of charge.

◆ Dwarves and midgets have very little in common.

◆ If you can think of a better fish pun, let minnow.

- A man working in an orange juice factory was canned because he couldn't concentrate.

- Lately, I've been trying to touch my toes, which I don't find too complicated, but my knees can't get it straight.

- My friend's butler is missing his left arm, serves him right.

- If there was someone selling drugs at this place, weed know.

- I'm reading a book about anti-gravity and it's impossible to put down.

- If you don't like herb puns, you're going to have a bad thyme.

- It was an emotional wedding, even the cake was in tiers.

- I changed the name of my I-pod to Titanic; it's syncing now.

- Atheism is a non-prophet organization.

- I submitted 10 puns into a pun contest hoping one would win, but no pun in ten did.

- A garage sale is actually a garbage sale but the 'b' is silent.

- A Buddhist walks up to a hotdog stand and says, "Make me one with everything."

- When a song writer dies, they decompose.

- Originally, I didn't like my beard, but then it grew on me.

- Sarcasm is lost on kleptomaniacs because they always take things literally.

- Someone stole my Microsoft Office account and they're going to pay, you have my Word.

- We have a genetic disposition for diarrhea, it runs in our jeans.

- I tried to catch fog yesterday, but I mist.

- To the handicapped guy who stole my bag: You can hide but you can't run.
- I took the shell off of my racing snail, thinking it would make him faster, but it turns out it only made him more sluggish.
- Someone stole my mood ring, I don't know how to feel about it.
- Fixing broken windows is such a pane.
- The first rule about Alzheimer's Club is don't talk about Chess Club.
- Skeletons are always calm because nothing gets under their skin.
- A motorcycle gang made up of ancient bisexual norse monarchs: The Bikings.
- As I suspected, someone has been adding soil to my garden; the plot thickens.
- Velcro is such a rip-off.
- Your gene pool could use a little chlorine.
- Jokes about German Sausage are the wurst.
- A war between two planets: A world war.
- A soldier who survived mustard gas and pepper spray is now a seasoned veteran.
- I know a guy who is addicted to brake fluid but he says he can stop anytime.
- I stayed up all night to see where the sun went, then it dawned on me.
- This girl said she recognized me from the vegetarian club, but I'd never met herbivore.
- I did a theatrical performance on puns, it was a play on words.
- They told me I have Type A blood but it was a Type O.
- PMS jokes aren't funny, period.

- I hate how funerals are at like 9 or 10 AM because I'm not a mourning person.
- There is a class trip to the Coca-Cola factory, I hope there is no pop quiz.
- Energizer bunny arrested: Charged with battery.
- When you get a bladder infection, urine trouble.
- I once offered a teddy bear dinner but he said, "No thanks, I'm already stuffed."
- People say filling your animals with helium is wrong, but I say, "Whatever floats your goat."
- I love donuts because they are not self-centered at all.
- I'm terrified of elevators, so I'll be taking steps to avoid them.
- I wondered why the ball kept getting bigger and then it hit me.
- Dull pencils are pointless.
- Time flies like an arrow and fruit flies like a banana.
- Shout out to people who are wondering what the opposite of in is.
- A cannibal is someone who is fed up with people.
- When my wife told me to stop impersonating a flamingo, I had to put my foot down.
- Yesterday, a clown held the door for me and I thought it was a nice jester.
- Any salad can be a Caesar Salad if you stab it enough.
- Yes I am carrying my house, but don't worry because it's a lighthouse.
- For sale: Parachute, only used once, never opened.
- I'm not really a fan of archery because it has too many drawbacks.
- Shout out to uteruses, the original 3-D printers.

- The USA is having so many disasters and tragedies, you'd almost think it was built on thousands of ancient burial grounds.

- A man got hit in the head with a soda but it's all right because it was a soft drink.

- If you ever feel like running around naked, just spray yourself with windex because it prevents streaking.

- In my spare time I like to make cheese puns; it's probably why I'm provolone.

- Stealing someone's coffee is called mugging.

- Pasteurize: Too far to see.

- Whoever invented knock-knock jokes should get a no-bell prize.

- No matter how much you push the envelope, it will still be stationary.

- I put my grandma on speed dial, I call that insta-gram.

- Dogs can't operate an MRI machine, but catscan.

- I'm glad that I know sign language; it's pretty handy.

- If attacked by a mob of clowns, go for the juggler.

- I get angry when my cell phone's battery dies so my therapist said I should find a good outlet.

- I'm a social vegan; I avoid meet.

- The key to a good mailman joke is the delivery.

- Rest in peace boiling water, you will be mist.

- I hate Russian Nesting Dolls; they are so full of themselves.

- Jesus drove a Honda but didn't talk about it, "For I did not speak of my own accord." - John 12:49

- A man walked into his home and was absolutely delighted when he discovered that someone had stolen every lamp in his house.

- I spilled spot remover on my dog and now he's gone.

- People are making apocalypse jokes like there's no tomorrow.

- I replaced my shoelaces with headphones and now I never have to worry about them coming untied again.

- I bought my friend an elephant for their room, they said, "Thank you." and I said, "Don't mention it."

- If someone farts at a poker tournament, you'll never know who did it.

- The past tense of fit should be fat.

- You know what they say about a will... It's a dead giveaway.

- I'm so sick of people thinking they can just waltz into my room when I'm obviously listening to my music in 4/4.

- I ate some food coloring and dyed a little on the inside.

- If your parents don't have children, chances are you won't either.

- If you were dating an FBI agent and you broke up, he'd be your Fedex.

- A war between two fridges: A cold war.

- I don't trust stairs because they are always up to something.

- The most used piece of equipment at the gym is the mirror.

- Singing in the shower is all fun and games until you get soap in your mouth, then it becomes a soap opera.

- The invention of the shovel was groundbreaking, but the invention of the broom really swept the nation.

- Poop jokes aren't my favorite kind of jokes, but they are a solid number two.

- Being cremated is my last hope for a smoking hot body.

- Police station toilet stolen; cops have nothing to go on.

- It's not a true communism joke unless everyone gets it.

- A blind man walked into a bar, then a table, then a chair.

- My grandfather has the heart of a lion and a lifetime ban from the zoo.

- My friend David had his I.D. Stolen, now we just call him Dav.

- If anyone asks you to spell part backwards, don't do it, it's a trap.

- I attached all of my watches together to make a belt, it was a waist of time.

- I let a pasta chef borrow my car, but then he returned it al dente.

- Two wrongs don't make a right, but two Wrights make an airplane.

- A magician was walking down the street and turned into a grocery store.

- I broke up with my gym because we just weren't working out.

- I never wanted to believe my dad was stealing from his job as a construction worker, but when I got home all the signs were there.

- A violin and a viola are just fiddling around.

- Apparently someone in London gets stabbed every 52 seconds, poor guy.

- If you ever get cold, just go stand in a corner, they're usually around 90 degrees.

- I think I want a job cleaning mirrors because it's something I could see myself doing.

- I opened a company selling landmines that look like prayer mats, now Prophets are going through the roof.

- I farted in my wallet and now I have gas money.

- I had a little bird, her name was Enza, I opened up the window and influenza.

- I used to be a lifeguard but this blue kid got me fired.

- Two drums and a cymbal fell off a cliff: Ba-Dum-Tssss.

- We had a contest at work for the best neckwear, and it was a tie.

- I went to the zoo the other day, and it was empty except for a single dog; it was a shitzu.

- The tombstones on the left were identical to the ones on the right; he was buried in the middle of the symmetry.

- We should all give the utmost respect to organ donors because it takes guts to do what they do.

- 5000 hares have escaped from the zoo; the police are combing the area.

- Mountains aren't just funny, they are hill areas.

- Every year, hundreds of children are shipped off to mime school, never to be heard from again.

- I watched a movie about pollution, and it was anti-climatic.

- When the cannibal showed up late to the luncheon, they gave him the cold shoulder.

- I don't trust people with graph paper because they're always plotting something.

- I broke my finger today but on the other hand, I am completely fine.

- Old people at weddings always poke me and say, "You are next," so I started doing the same thing at funerals.

- Instead of "The John", I call my toilet "The Jim" that way it sounds better when I say I go to "The Jim" first thing every morning.

- When you're gay in your house with nobody else, you're homolone.

- I tell dad jokes but I have no kids so I'm a faux pa.

- You've really got to hand it to short people, because they usually can't reach it anyway.
- I just swapped our bed for a trampoline; my wife's going to hit the roof.
- I just called the library to make a reservation but couldn't because they were completely booked.
- I hate people who talk about me behind my back; they discussed me.
- Shout out to my grandma, that's the only way she can hear.
- I just ate a frozen apple; it was hardcore.
- Tomorrow is Jamaican hairstyle day and I'm dreading it.
- I just bought a thesaurus and when I got it home I found out that all the pages are blank; I have no words to describe how angry I am.
- Tennis players grunt too much when they play, there is no need for all that racquet.
- I've just qualified as an archaeologist and now I find my life is in ruins.
- Scientists believe that most people lean forward slightly when they nod their head. I'm inclined to agree.
- I used to be a narcissist, but look at me now.
- I saw a documentary last night about how old ships are held together and I found it quite riveting.
- I used to have a job as a can crusher, but I had to quit because It was just soda-pressing.
- Haunted french pancakes give me the crepes.
- Birthdays are good for your health; studies show that people who have more birthdays live the longest.
- I have a condition that makes me eat when I can't sleep called insom-nom-nom-nom-nia.
- I always see the shadiest people sitting under trees.

- Most people have 32 teeth and some have 10, it's simple meth

- The experienced carpenter really nailed it, but the new guy screwed everything up.

- I used to be addicted to soap, but I'm clean now.

- When William joined the army, he disliked the phrase 'fire at will'.

- My friend's bakery burned down last night, now his business is toast.

- Broken puppets for sale, no strings attached.

- Two peanuts were walking in a tough neighborhood and one of them was a-salted.

- Novice pirates make terrible singers because they can't hit the high seas.

- Sleeping comes so naturally to me, I could do it with my eyes closed.

- There was a big paddle sale at the boat store, it was quite the oar deal.

- No one knew she had a dental implant until it came out in a conversation.

- Don't trust people who do acupuncture; they are back stabbers.

- I saw a beaver movie last night, it was the best dam movie I've ever seen.

- He drove his expensive car into a tree and found out how the Mercedes bends.

- I was struggling to figure out how lightning works, then it struck me.

- The magician got so mad he pulled his hare out.

- I once heard a joke about amnesia, but I forgot how it goes.

- I used to be a banker, but I lost interest.

- I lost my paper towels, I think I need a bounty hunter.

- A prisoner's favorite punctuation mark is the period because it marks the end of his sentence.

- I was going to look for my watch but I could never find the time.

- Eating a clock is very time-consuming.

- I knew a woman who owned a taser, man was she stunning.

- I tried to look up impotence on the internet but nothing came up.

- I was going to buy a book on phobias, but I was afraid it wouldn't help me.

- I think Santa has riverfront property in Brazil because all our presents came from Amazon this year.

- Some people's noses and feet are built backwards: their feet smell and their noses run.

- I try wearing tight jeans, but I can never pull them off.

- A hole has been found in the nudist camp wall; the police are looking into it.

- I used to have a fear of hurdles, but I got over it.

- People are choosing cremation over traditional burial, it shows that people are thinking outside the box.

- Show me a piano falling down a mineshaft and I'll show you A-flat minor.

- To the guy who invented zero, thanks for nothing.

- I caught my neighbor stealing my red food dye, when he was caught red handed, he said, "I'm gonna dye".

- My aunt loves telling stupid jokes while she knits; she is a real knitwit.

- Smaller babies may be delivered by stork, but the heavier ones need a crane.

- Becoming a vegetarian is a huge missed stake.

- I threw a boomerang at a ghost last week, I knew it'd come back to haunt me.

- I went to the Air and Space Museum but there was nothing there.

- As a scarecrow, people say I'm outstanding in my field, but, hey, It's in my jeans.

- Sometimes I tuck my knees into my chest; It's just how I roll... Forward.

- I totally understand how batteries feel because I'm rarely included in things either.

- I buy all my guns from a guy called "T-Rex", he's a small arms dealer.

- Looking back, John's orange soda fetish is kinda weird, wonder what his Fanta-sies were.

- A farmer in his field with his cows counted 196, but when he rounded them up, he had 200.

- If you want to catch a squirrel, just climb a tree and act like a nut.

- Thieves have broken into my house and stolen everything except for my soap, shower gel, deodorant, and towel... Dirty bastards.

- I couldn't figure out how to work my seatbelt, then it clicked.

- I can't believe I got fired from the calendar factory, all I did was take a day off.

- Don't fart in an Apple Store because they don't have windows.

- I love the rotation of the earth because it really makes my day.

- I ate too much Middle Eastern food, now I falafel.

- I serve my eggs Benedict on a golden platter because there's no plates like gold for the Hollandaise.

- I hated my job at the fireworks factory, I got fired a lot.

- There was an explosion at a cheese factory in France; there was de-Brie everywhere.

- A pet store had a bird contest, no perches necessary.

- The furniture store keeps calling me to come back, but all I wanted was one night stand.

- I just found out that I'm colorblind, the diagnosis came completely out of the purple.

- I saw an ad for burial plots, and thought to myself this is the last thing I need.

- A termite walks into a bar and says, "Where is the bar tender?"

- I have a few jokes about unemployed people but it doesn't matter because none of them work.

- eBay is so useless, I tried to look up lighters and all they had was 17,282 matches.

- I wasn't originally going to get a brain transplant, but then I changed my mind.

- I was addicted to the hokey pokey, but I turned myself around.

- A courtroom artist was arrested today for an unknown reason; the details are kinda sketchy.

- I am so poor I can't even pay attention.

- A friend of mine tried to annoy me with bird puns, but I soon realized that toucan play at that game.

- I hate insect puns because they really bug me.

- I'm taking part in a stair climbing competition, I guess I'd better step up my game.

- Claustrophobic people are more productive thinking outside the box.

- The best time to open a gift is the present.

- I just burned 2,000 calories, so I guess that's the last time I leave brownies in the oven while I nap.

- I would make jokes about the sea, but they are too deep.
- I used to work at a fire hydrant factory, and I couldn't even park near the place.
- I wanted to make a joke about criminals, but I was scared it would get stolen.
- I can't throw the ball, it keeps bouncing away; this situation is getting out of hand.
- I would tell a history joke, but they're too old fashioned.
- A Roman fighter consumed his wife, and then said he was gladiator.
- I don't know if I just got hit by frozen rain but it hurt like hail.
- The girl quit her job at the doughnut factory because she was fed up with the hole business.
- The first time I used an elevator it was really uplifting, but then it let me down.
- The butcher backed up into the meat grinder and got a little behind in his work.
- The Balloon family name died when it ran out of heir.
- I really wanted a camouflage shirt but I couldn't find one.
- I don't get how people stumble into mirrors; they need to watch themselves.
- A quarter-acre of underdeveloped land may not seem like much to some people, but to me it's a lot.
- I knew a guy who collected candy canes, they were all in mint condition.
- I told my wife that it was her turn to shovel and salt the front steps, but all I got was icy stares.
- If towels could tell jokes, they would probably have a dry sense of humor.

Pirate Jokes (Rated ARRR)

Obscene? Perhaps. Disturbing? Maybe. Inappropriate? Probably. Funny? Absolutely. This section isn't for general audiences, it's not for children. Prepare yourself for naughty language and privates parts, lots of them.

- What do a cheap hotel and skinny jeans have in common? There's no ball room.

- How do you spot a blind man at a nudist colony? It's not hard.

- Why didn't Barbie ever get pregnant? Because Ken came in another box.

- I once swallowed two pieces of string and they came out tied together. I shit you knot.

- A pirate walks into a bar with a steering wheel on the front of his pants. The bartender says to him, "That looks pretty painful." The pirate replies, "Aye. It's driving me nuts."

- Why can't Miss Piggy count to 100? When she gets to 69 she gets a frog in her throat.

- People who say they are constipated are full of shit.

- They used to be called jumpolines until your mom jumped on one.

- What hangs at a man's thigh and wants to poke the hole that it's often poked before? A key.

- If someone threw a rock and knocked you off your donkey, would you be considered stoned off your ass?

- Did you hear about the paperboy that got caught masturbating at work? It's all over the news.

- Friends are like condoms. They protect you when things get hard.

- Did you hear about the chameleon that couldn't change color? He had reptile dysfunction.

- What kind of shoes does a pedophile wear? White vans.

- A leaf and an emo fall from a tree. Which hits the ground first? The leaf. The rope stops the emo.

- It's not that the man didn't know how to juggle. It's just that he didn't have the balls to do it.

- Thank God for nipples. Without them, boobs would be pointless.

- Are you from Europe? Because europiece of shit.

- There was a blind man walking down the street with a stick. He walked past this fish market, stopped, took a deep breath, and said, "Wooo. Good morning ladies."

- Australians don't have sex. Australians mate.

- Why was the pedophile late for work? He was lollygagging.

- Is it wrong to tell a "your mom" joke to an orphan?

- What plant has the most sex? A rosebush. It's always thorny.

- What's the worst thing about being a pedophile? Just trying to fit in.

- Why is Santa's sack so big? Because he only comes once a year.

- If you were a vegetable you would be a cabbitch.

- Life is like toilet paper. You're either on a roll or taking shit from an asshole.

- Some rubbers help erase mistakes. Some rubbers prevent them from happening.

- What's the difference between a hooker and a drug dealer? A hooker can wash her crack and sell it again.

- What's the difference between snowmen and snow-women? Snowballs

- Over the past year, my sexual fetishes had been getting slowly more perverse; But it wasn't until I spanked a statue that I realized I'd hit rock bottom.

- What idiot called it "leaving after sex" and not "nuts and bolts"?

- Why was the guitar teacher arrested? For fingering a minor.

- What's long and hard and full of semen? Submarines.

- What did the hurricane say to the coconut tree? "Hold onto your nuts, this is no ordinary blow job."

- What's the difference between deer nuts and beer nuts? Beer nuts are $1.75 but deer nuts are under a buck.

- I'm emotionally constipated. I haven't given a shit in days.

- What's long and hard and has cum in it? Cucumber.

- Love is like a machine. Sometimes you need a good screw to fix it.

- I'm trying to finish writing a script for a porno movie, but there are just too many holes in the plot.

- Why was the snowman smiling? Because the snowblower was coming.

- Have you ever tried having sex while camping? It's fucking in tents.

- What do you call a lesbian dinosaur? Lickalotopus.

- What's a 6.9? Another good thing screwed up by a period.

- What's the difference between a pregnant woman and a lightbulb? You can unscrew a lightbulb.

- What do you call a herd of cows masturbating? Beef strokin' off.

Jokes That'll Get You Extra Credit

If you don't understand these jokes, maybe you should go back to school. These might require some serious brainpower, which could be asking a lot from you. So, put your thinking caps on, this could get strenuous. Mentally I mean, in case, ya know, that wasn't clear. All I'm saying is, go slowly here and remember that Google is your friend.

- Helium walks into a bar and orders a beer. The bartender says, "Sorry, we don't serve noble gases here." He doesn't react.

- How many surrealists does it take to screw in a light bulb? A fish.

- There's a band called 1023 MB. They haven't had any gigs yet.

- What happens when you hear 1,000 Polish jokes? They just get Warsaw and Warsaw.

- When chemists die, we barium.

- When she told me I was average, she was just being mean.

- Another name for Santa's elves: Subordinate clauses.

- They say a Freudian Slip is when you say one thing but you really mean your mother.

- What do you say in order to comfort an upset grammar nazi? There, their, they're.

- Sodium, sodium, sodium, sodium, sodium, sodium, sodium, sodium, Batman.

- What do you get when you cross a joke with a rhetorical question?

- What is a physicist's favorite food? Fission chips.

- C, E flat, and G walk into a bar and the bartender says, "Sorry, no minors."

- What do you get when you put root beer in a square glass? Beer.

- Two kittens are on a sloped roof. Which one falls off first? The one with the lowest mew.

- A biologist, a chemist, and a statistician are out hunting. The biologist shoots at a deer and misses 5 feet to the left. The chemist takes a shot and misses 5 feet to the right. The statistician shouts, "We got one!"

- Parallel lines have so much in common. It's a shame they'll never meet.

- A physicist sees a young man about to jump off the Empire State Building. He yells, "Don't do it! You have so much potential!"

- A hot blonde walks into a bar and orders a double entendre at the bar. The bartender gave it to her.

- Where do German chemists put their dirty dishes? In the Zinc.

- How many potatoes does it take to kill an Irish man? None.

- What happens if you swallow uranium? You get atomic ache.

- If electricity always follows the path of least resistance, why doesn't lightning only strike in France?

- Which way does a cyclops wing their eyeliner? It doesn't matter because Nobody is going to criticize their makeup.

- Did you know Type O blood was actually Type Zero blood due to the lack of glycoproteins in the blood. But it was misread and is now Type O blood. I guess you could call it a typo.

- You know how there's a theory that no two people see color the same? Does that mean color is a pigment of our imagination?

- What natural disaster is best at stopping communism? A torNATO.

- My new joke on inertia doesn't seem to be gaining any momentum.

- Why is Oedipus against profanity? Because he kisses his mother with that mouth.

- The past, the present, and the future walk into a bar. It was tense.

- How often do I make chemistry jokes? Periodically.

- I blew up my chemistry experiment. Oxidants happen.

- Where does bad light end up? In prism.

- Why did the chemist's pants keep falling down? He had no acetol.

- The math teacher was a good dancer, so much algorithm.

- You matter, until you multiply yourself times the speed of light squared. Then you energy.

- What do you call an acid with an attitude? A-mean-oh acid.

- "I've got 95 problems and the catholic churches sale of indulgences are all of them." - Martin Luther, probably

- What do you call a man who spent all summer at the beach? Tangent.

- What do you say when you see an empty parrot cage? Polygon.

- What do you call a crushed angle? A rectangle.

- What did the Italian say when the witch doctor removed the curse? Hexagon.

- What did the little acorn say when he grew up? Geometry.

- What do you call an angle that's adorable? Acute angle.

- What line do you use to tie up a package? A Chord.

- What do you call a drawn, fierce beast? A line.

- What do you call more than one 'L'? A parallel.

- What do you call people who are in favor of tractors? Protractors.

- What should you do when it rains? Coincide.

- The lab smells like rotten eggs? Sorry to hear about your sulfuring.

- I accidentally froze myself to absolute zero but I'm 0K now.

- What kind of fish is made of only two sodium atoms? 2 Na.

- Are there anymore good chemistry jokes? I don't Zinc so.

- 6 was scared of 7 because 7, 8, 9, but why did 7 eat 9? Because you're supposed to eat 3 squared meals a day.

- You can tell the gender of an ant by throwing it in the water. If it sinks: girl ant. If it floats: buoyant.

- What does the military use acid for? To neutralize the enemy base.

- Einstein finally developed a theory about space and it was about time too.

- I walked down a street where the houses were numbered 64K, 128K, 256K, 512K, and 1MB. That was a trip down memory lane.

- Why did the capacitor kiss the diode? He just couldn't resistor.

- Why wasn't the geologist hungry? They'd lost their apatite.

- Just went to the grocery store and swapped my 50 raisins for 100 sultanas. I can't believe how good the currant exchange rate is.

- A Roman soldier walked into a bar, held up two fingers and said, "Five beers please."

- What did the cell say to his sister when she stepped on his foot? Mitosis.

- Schrödinger's cat walks into a bar and doesn't.

- A photon is checking into a hotel and the bellhop asks him, "Do you have any luggage?" The photon replies, "Nope, I'm traveling light."

- How do you know the moon is going broke? It's down to its last quarter.

- Why did the bear dissolve in water? It was polar.

- Two chemists walk into a bar. The first says, "I'll have some H2O." The second says, "I'll have some H2O too." The second one dies.

- What do you call an educated tube? A graduated cylinder.

- Why can't you trust atoms? They make up everything.

- The roundest knight at king Arthur's round table was Sir Cumfrence.

- You can't plant flowers if you haven't botany.

- Did you hear about the guy who jumped off a bridge in Paris? He was in seine.

- What's the worst thing about ancient orators? They tend to Babylon.

- I made a graph of my past relationships. It has an ex axis and a why axis.

- Atheists don't solve exponential equations because they don't believe in higher powers.

- Alphabet soup? More like Times New Ramen.

- I found a rock yesterday which measured 1760 yards in length. Must be some kind of milestone.

- There's safety in numbers, but I prefer Deuteronomy.

- An opinion without 3.14159 is just an onion.

- Cells multiply by dividing.

- What do computers eat for a snack? Microchips.

- Never discuss infinity with a mathematician. They can go on forever.

- Why does the Norwegian navy have barcodes on the side of their ships? So when they arrive back in port, they can Scandinavian.

- Two atoms are walking along. One of them says, "Oh no! I think we lost an electron." The other asked, "Are you sure?" and the first responded, "Yes, I'm positive."

- An infectious disease walks into a bar. The barman says, "We don't serve your type here." The disease replies, "Well you're not a very good host."

- There are 10 types of people in this world: those who understand binary and those who don't.

- What does a subatomic duck say? Quark.

- What do you call two crows on a branch? Attempted murder.

- Why did Karl Marx dislike Earl Grey Tea? Because all proper tea is theft.

- Descartes walks into a bar. The bartender asks him if he wants a drink. Descartes says, "I think not," and then he disappears.

- A superconductor walks into a bar and orders a beer. The bartender tells him to get out. The superconductor puts up no resistance.

- A train operator shocked himself and he was completely fine. Why? He was a bad conductor.

- A photon walks into two bars.

Pickup Lines

You're at a bar. All your lines and tricks you've spent years accumulating to bring to social gatherings such as this, just aren't working. You're stuck. All hope seems lost. Until... A light appears. You've stumbled upon this section of jokes (because you're the kind of person who brings a joke book to a bar) and you find the one. The line of all lines. The line that will make your target swoon and collapse into your arms.

- You must be the speed of light because time stops when I look at you.

- Do you have a name or can I call you mine?

- Roses are red, violets are blue, I didn't know what perfect was until I met you.

- I'm no organ donor, but I'd be happy to give you my heart.

- Are you a fisherman? Because I think you're a reel catch.

- You want to know what my shirt is made out of? Boyfriend material.

- I'm not a hoarder but I really want to keep you forever.

- Is your body from McDonald's? Because I'm lovin' it.

- Do you believe in love at first sight or should I walk by again?

- Are you a magician? Because when I look at you, everyone else disappears.

- Do you have a band-aid? Because I scrapped my knees falling for you.

- Are you religious? Because you are the answer to all of my prayers.

- Your lips look so lonely, would they like to meet mine?

- You must be a hell of a thief because you stole my heart from across the room.

- You must have died recently because you look like an angel.

- Is your dad a preacher? Because you are a blessing.

- Are you a camera? Because every time I look at you I smile.

- There's only one thing I want to change about you: Your last name.

- You look familiar. Didn't we take a class together? I could have sworn we had chemistry.

- Are you from the Netherlands? Because Amsterdam.

- Are those space pants? Because your butt is out of this world.

- You remind me of an overdue library book because you've got fine written all over you.

- Do you have a shovel in your pocket? Because I'm digging that ass.

- Tonight, this Han doesn't want to fly solo.

- On a scale of 1 to 10: You're a 9 and I'm the one you need.

- You are hotter than the bottom of my laptop.

- Can I borrow a kiss? I promise I'll give it back.

- Do you have a map? Because I keep getting lost in your eyes.

- You better call life alert, because I've fallen for you and can't get up.

- When God made you, he was showing off.

- Do you mind if I walk you home? My mother always said to follow your dreams.

- Do you have an inhaler? You took my breath away.

- I don't believe in love at first sight but I'm willing to make an exception in your case.

- You know what's beautiful? Read the first word.

- If I was an octopus, all 3 of my hearts would beat for you.
- I should call you Google because you have everything I'm looking for.
- Pizza is my second favorite thing to eat in bed.
- Are you a trampoline? Because I want to bounce on you.
- I lost my teddy bear. Can I sleep with you?
- Are you a mirror? Because I can see myself inside you.
- Do you want to go on a ate? I'll give you the D later.
- You must be Medusa because you make me rock hard.
- You're so hot, I could roast my meat on you.
- You know how your hair would look really good? In my lap.
- Let's play Barbie. I'll be Ken and you can be the box I come in.
- You're like my little toe, because I'm going to bang you on every piece of furniture in my home.
- You look ill. You must be suffering from a lack of vitamin Me.
- Are you a Disney princess? Because you're cinder-hella fine.
- You look so innocent, you look so sweet, as long as I have a face, you'll always have a seat.
- Are your legs made of butter? Because I'd like to spread them.
- Would you like to try an Australian kiss? It's like a French kiss but down under.
- The only thing I want between our relationship is latex.
- Sit on my lap and we'll get things straight between us.
- I'm like a Rubik's cube. The more you play with me, the harder I get.

- Are you a tortilla? Because I want to flip you over and eat you out.

- I might not go down in history, but I'll go down on you.

- I like every bone in your body, especially mine.

- I'm no weather man, but you can expect a few inches tonight.

- Sex is evil; evil is sin; sin is forgiven, so let's begin.

- There are 8 planets in the universe, but only 7 after I destroy Uranus.

- I'll treat you like my homework: slam you on the table and do you all night long.

- My bed is broken. Can I sleep in yours?

- You're so hot, even my zipper is falling for you.

- Don't worry, I played Tetris as a kid. I can make it fit.

- Are you a scientist? Because I want to do you on a table, periodically.

- The word of the day is legs. Would you like to go back to my place to spread the word?

- That shirt is really becoming on you, but you know, if I were on you, I'd be coming too.

- Save water, shower with me.

- You are on my list of things to do tonight.

- Lets play Titanic. You can be the iceberg and I'll go down on you.

- I've got the ship. You've got the harbor. Why don't we tie up for the night?

- If your left leg is Christmas and your right leg is Thanksgiving, can I visit you in between the holidays?

- Do you like jigsaw puzzles? Would you like to go back to my place and put our pieces together?

- Are you my new boss? Because you just gave me a raise.

Anti-Jokes

These jokes aren't funny. Don't get your hopes up. This is a rough section. It takes guts to push through. **Good luck** (You'll need it).

- What do you get when you cross a railway with a fridge? Dead.
- What's red and bad for your teeth? A brick.
- What's green and fuzzy and would probably kill you if it fell from a tree? A pool table.
- What's big red and eats rocks? A big red rock eater.
- What do you call a dog with no legs? It doesn't matter. It's not going to come anyway.
- What's red and smells like blue paint? Red paint.
- Why can't the T-Rex clap? Because it's dead.
- Why did Sally fall off the swings? Because she didn't have any arms. Knock-knock. Who's there? Not Sally.
- What leaves a bigger memory than a passionate kiss? A stab wound.
- What do you call a man with a shovel in his head? An ambulance because he has a rather serious injury.
- What ended in 1896? 1895.
- How many apples grow on a tree? All of them.
- Where was the Declaration of Independence signed? At the bottom.
- Which side of the cheetah has the most spots? The outside.
- Why do you never see elephants hiding in trees? Because they are really good at it.
- What's white and can't climb trees? A fridge.
- What sport do you play with a wombat? Wom.

- Yo mama so fat she should be concerned because diabetes is a serious problem.

- A man walks into a bar. His alcohol dependency is tearing his family apart.

- What's worse than finding a worm in your apple? The holocaust.

- What did the girl say when she got stung by a bee? Nothing, she was allergic.

- What's red and moves up and down? A tomato in an elevator.

- What did the farmer say when he lost his tractor? "Where's my tractor?"

- What did one Japanese man say to the other? I don't know. I can't speak Japanese.

- Why did the man fall into the well? He was visually impaired.

- What's brown and sticky? A stick.

- A duck walks into a bar, the bartender says, "What'll it be?" The duck says nothing because it's a duck.

- I still remember the last words of my grandfather before he kicked the bucket. He said, "Hey, how far do you think I can kick this bucket?"

- Friends are a lot like snow. If you pee on them, they disappear.

- Where do you find a dog with no legs? Right where you left him.

- Never criticize someone until you've walked a mile in their shoes, that way when you do, you'll be a mile away and have their shoes.

- What did the boy say when he dropped his ice cream? Nothing, he was hit by a bus.

- A dyslexic man walked into a bra.

- A horse walked into a bar. Several people got up and left as they spotted the potential danger in the situation.

- If life throws you melons, you might be dyslexic.

- Why did the chicken commit suicide? To get to the other side.

- What do you call a fish with no eye? Fsh.

- Did you hear about the man who ran in front of a bus? He got tired.

- What does Santa give naughty kids for Christmas? Nothing, he doesn't exist.

- What's worse than being bitten by a snake? Being bitten twice.

- What did Batman say to Robin before they got in the Bat-mobile? "Get in the Bat-mobile."

- A dog walks into a bar because someone left the door open.

- Did you know that Hellen Keller had a swing set? Neither did she.

- What's green and has wheels? Grass. I lied about the wheels.

- Why did the mushroom go to the party? It didn't. Fungus is not capable of having a social life.

- Every 60 seconds in Europe, a minute passes.

- Why can't snowmen get tan? Because snowflakes have no pigment and snow melts when exposed to high temperatures.

- A man walks into a bar. Now he needs stitches because he was walking pretty fast.

- How many electricians does it take to screw in a lightbulb? One.

- Do you know what really makes me smile? Facial muscles.

Jokes to be Thrown Away

The title of this section seems pretty self explanatory. So, uh, here you go.

- Throwing lamps at people who need to lighten up
- Throwing handles at people who need to get a grip
- Throwing refrigerators at people who need to chill
- Throwing scissors at people who need to cut it out
- Throwing clocks at people who need to get with the times
- Throwing matches at people who need to get fired up
- Throwing bridges at people who need to get over it
- Throwing demons at people for the hell of it
- Throwing brake fluid at people who need to stop
- Throwing coins at people who need to change
- Throwing keyboards at people who aren't your type
- Throwing rocks at people who are stoned
- Throwing rockets at people who are out of this world
- Throwing cheese at people who are grate
- Throwing laundry detergent at people who need to tide-y up
- Throwing cars at people who drive you crazy
- Throwing calendars at people you want to date
- Throwing dull pencils at people who are pointless
- Throwing ladders at people who need to step it up
- Throwing joysticks at people who need to control themselves
- Throwing fertilizer at people who need to grow up

- Throwing balls at people who need to just roll with it

- Throwing trees at people who need to leaf you alone

- Throwing straws at people who suck

- Throwing screwdrivers at people who need to loosen up

- Throwing spices at people who have no taste

- Throwing textbooks at people who need to learn a lesson

- Throwing vacuums at people who need to suck it up

- Throwing seeds at people who need to grow a pair

- Throwing doors at people who need to get out

- Throwing glue at people who need to stick to it

- Throwing laxatives at people who don't have their shit together

- Throwing circles at people you want to keep around

- Throwing skulls at people who need to get ahead in life

- Throwing paper at people who are tearable

- Throwing knives at people who aren't too sharp

- Throwing oceans at people who don't sea well

- Throwing donkeys at people who need to get off their ass

- Throwing windows at people who are a pane in your glass

- Throwing money at people who need to pay more attention

- Throwing bananas at people that you find appealing

- Throwing gyms at people who need to work it out

- Throwing cows at people who need to moooo-ve

Pop Culture

This section has nothing to do with soda, balloons, or Aborigines, you idiot. It's full of references and jokes about things only people who are fictionally inclined will understand. Or at least, anyone who hasn't been living under a rock for the past twenty years. Carry on.

- I started walking around without any shoes and it sort of became a Hobbit.

- Bilbo was surprised to wake one morning and find a Walmart had been built next to his house. It was an unexpected item in the Baggins area.

- What do you call a kid who can't find his Lord of the Rings toy? Lego-loss.

- A stormtrooper buys an iPhone because he couldn't find the droid he was looking for.

- I gotta say, Kylo Ren is my favorite Star Wars villain, Han's down.

- Why did the angry Jedi cross the road? To get to the Dark Side.

- What do you call Harrison Ford when he smokes weed? Han So-high.

- What do you call a potato that has turned to the Dark Side? Vader Tots.

- Why did episodes 4, 5, and 6 of Star Wars come before 1, 2, and 3? Because in charge of planning, Yoda was.

- Doctor Octopus robbed a bank the other day. He didn't have a gun, but he was well armed.

- Where does Superman park his privates? On Lois Lane.

- What is it called when batman leaves church early? Christian Bail.

- What does batman get in his drinks? Just ice.

- What happens when Batman sees Catwoman? The Dark Knight rises.

- Superman is really good at being a superhero. He can do it on the fly.

- What do you call security guards working outside Samsung shops? Guardians of the Galaxy.

- They should put an advertisement on the Hulk because he's basically a giant banner.

- Harry Potter can't tell the difference between his cooking pot and his best mate. They're both cauldron.

- How did Harry Potter get down the hill? Walking... J. K. Rowling.

- On a scale of one to ten, how obsessed with Harry Potter are you? About nine and three quarters.

- How do Death Eaters freshen their breath? With dementos.

- It's hard to tell from most angles, but Spock actually has three ears: the left ear, the right ear, and the final front ear.

- What did Mark Wahlberg feed Ted? Nothing. He was already stuffed.

- Why can't you give Elsa a balloon? Because she will Let it go.

- Did you hear that Clint Eastwood opened a preschool? It's called "Go Ahead and Make My Day Care Center".

- Why was Dewey Finn walking hard? He got some Tenacious D.

- Why couldn't Dorothy tell the difference between the bad witch and the good witch? Because she couldn't tell which witch was which.

- What do you get when you cross Sonic the Hedgehog and Curious George? 2 Fast 2 Curious.

- How does Reese eat ice cream? Witherspoon.

- Did you hear about the new Johnny Depp movie? It's the one rated Arrrrrrr.

- What do you get when you cross a robot and a tractor? A Transfarmer.

- If Peeta were a ginger, would he be called the gingerbread man?

- What do you call Watson when Sherlock isn't around? Holmeless.

- I used to go fishing with Skrillex but he kept dropping the bass.

- Matthew McConaughey's Lincoln can't make left turns. It just goes all right, all right, all right.

- I asked a French man if he played video games. He said, "Wii."

- Dr. Frankenstein entered a bodybuilding competition and discovered he had seriously misunderstood the objective.

- What did Dr. Frankenstein say about his dog's drool? "It's saallivaaa".

- Liam Neeson struggles with being unappreciated after saving his family. Taken 4: Granted.

- What's Forrest Gump's password? 1Forrest1.

- In the lego universe, all doctors are plastic surgeons.

- Rick Astley will let you borrow any movie in his Pixar collection except one. He's never gonna give you Up.

- Research shows 6 out of 7 dwarves aren't happy.

- "Sorry I'm late. I got held up" - Simba

- Why was Tigger looking in the toilet? He was searching for Pooh.

- What does Olaf eat for lunch? Icebergers.

- What does Ariel like on her toast? Mermalade.

- What's Mickey Mouse's favorite sport? Minnie-golf.

- Why did Sleepy take firewood to bed with him? He wanted to sleep like a log.

- Why is Peter Pan always flying? Because he neverlands.

- What do you call a fairy who hasn't showered in years? Stinker Bell.

- A young deer in the woods learned to use all four hooves equally well. He was known to be bambidextrous.

- I asked the lion in my wardrobe what he was doing there. He said, "It's Narnia business."

- Why was Cinderella kicked off the basketball team? Because she ran away from the ball.

- My friend told me that I need to stop singing "I'm A Believer" because it was getting annoying. I laughed, thinking she was kidding, then I saw her face.

- My girlfriend told me she was leaving me because I kept pretending to be a Transformer. I said, "No wait! I can change."

- My computer's got Miley Virus because it has stopped twerking.

- I was so sad when I lost my playstation 3. Unfortunately, there was nobody there to console me.

- What did Zelda tell Link when he couldn't open the door? Triforce.

- How do you get Pikachu onto the bus? You Pokémon.

- I would tell a joke about Shrek, but they are too ogre-used.

- How do you find Will Smith in the snow? Look for fresh prints.

- What's Whitney Houston's favorite type of coordination? HAAAAAND EYEEEEEEEE.

- Why does Snoop Dogg carry an umbrella? Fo' drizzle.

- What do you call people who are afraid of Santa Clause? Claustrophobic.

- Why did Santa go to college for music? To improve his wrapping skills.

- What kind of overalls does Mario wear? Denim denim denim.

- What time does Sean Connery get to Wimbledon? Tennish.

- What do you do for a turtle who was falling in love, but now is only falling apart? There is nothing you can do, it's a turtle eclipse of the heart.

More Jokes

It takes a lot of work to organize all these jokes and keep track of them, so here are just some extra jokes that didn't belong in the other sections. They are still funny, don't get me wrong, it's just that I'm a bit lazy and I won't be taking the time to divide these up any further. Enjoy. Or don't... I'm just kidding, you definitely will.

- I lost my watch at a party once. I saw a guy stepping on it while sexually harassing a girl so I walked up to the dude and punched him in the nose. No one does that to a girl, not on my watch.

- A woman had twins and gave them up for adoption. One went to a family in Egypt and was named Amal and the other went to a family in Spain and was named Juan. Years later Juan sent a picture of himself to his birth mother. Upon receiving the picture, she told her husband that she wished she had a picture of Amal. He responded, "They're twins. Once you've seen Juan, you've seen Amal."

- How to be cool:

    A) use cool sunglasses emoji

    B)

- *Names child butter* *Brings home wrong child* I can't believe it's not butter!

- I told my friend she was drawing her eyebrows too high. She looked surprised.

- Boy scout: Sir, the lads and I found a snake. Is it poisonous?

    Leader: No, this snake isn't poisonous at all.

    One of them picks up the snake and it bites them. He begins to spasm and foam at the mouth.

    Leader: However, this snake is venomous. Venom is injected, poison is ingested or absorbed through the skin. Let's get it right next time lads.

- He texted me 'Your adorable' and I replied, 'No, you're adorable.' Now he likes me and all I did was point out a typo.

- A Mexican magician tells the audience he will disappear on the count of 3. He says, "Uno, Dos,..." and disappears without a tres.

- A little girl grows up thinking all doors are automatic, but actually, she's haunted by a really polite ghost. So chivalry really is dead.

- Someone told me my clothes were gay. I told them, "Well, of course. They came out of the closet this morning."

- My sister bet me 100 dollars that I couldn't make a car completely out of spaghetti. You should have seen the look on her face as I drove pasta.

- Eyelashes are supposed to prevent things from getting into your eyes, but when I do have something in my eye it's always and eyelash. Eyeronic.

- Two antennas met on a roof, fell in love, and got married. The ceremony was nothing special but the reception was great.

- A man died today when a pile of books fell onto him. He had only his shelf to blame.

- The shoemaker did not deny his apprentice anything he needed. He gave his awl.

- Two hats were hanging on a hat rack in the hallway. One hat says to the other, "You stay here, I'll go on a head."

- Two mice are chewing on a film roll. One of them goes, "I think the book was better."

- And the Lord said unto John, "Come fourth and receive eternal life." But John came fifth and won a toaster.

- I was walking through a quarry and said to the foreman, "That's a big rock!" "Boulder," he replied. So I puffed out my chest and shouted, "LOOK AT THAT ENOURMOUS ROCK OVER THERE!"

- My dad died when we couldn't remember his blood type. As he died, he kept insisting for us to "be positive", but it's hard without him here.

- "Doctor, there's a patient on line 1 that says he's invisible." "Well, tell him I can't see him right now."

- I wear two pairs of pants when I go golfing. People always ask me why I do. I say, "I wear two pants when I golf just in case I get a hole-in-one."

- A bus station is where a bus stops. A train station is where a train stops. On my desk, I have a work station.

- A small boy swallowed some coins and was then taken to a hospital. When his grandmother telephoned later to ask how he was, a nurse said, "No change yet."

- There is a special species of bird that is really good at holding stuff together. They are called velcrows.

- I was supposed to go to a funeral but ended up at the wrong cemetery. It was a grave error.

- Welcome to plastic surgery addicts anonymous. I'm seeing a lot of new faces and I have to say that I'm very disappointed.

- With all this talk of making Puerto Rico the 51st state, I feel like we should make a goal to get 53 states. A good solid prime number "One nation, Indivisible."

You're Finally Done

Congratulations! You've successfully made it through the whole book. If you're still actually reading this, you clearly enjoyed something.

Thank you for purchasing and reading my masterpiece! You're welcome for the new collection of jokes that you have in your hands. Thanks to me, you no longer have to aimlessly search through websites to find "funny" jokes. I think you've got all you need right here.

Again, if you found any of the stuff in this offensive, my work here is done. If you didn't understand or get some of these jokes, that's a real shame. If you know a joke that I didn't include, know that they probably just weren't funny enough to be included, because even though I don't have standards for my humor, a million pages does seem a little bit excessive.

Remember to treasure this work of art because it shall serve you well in your future, whether you're stuck at a holiday party and have nothing constructive to say, or your date decided (without telling you) that starting any conversation was your responsibility.

I would be sincerely appreciative if you gave this book an honest review. All you have to do is tell me exactly how this made you feel (fabulous, is the answer, I'm sure). It would help me tremendously, and let's be honest, at this point, I've given you so much. You might even owe me a review. Just honesty, that's all I need! Pleeeeeease.

Thank you in advance and have a nice day,

Rilee Ann

P.S.

I shall always continue searching for humor and adding to my ever growing collection. So, if you have some funny puns, pickup lines, or just any joke in general to share that you enjoy but didn't see while reading, send them to me! If you want. Perhaps you just wanted to praise me for my excellent work? Either way, you can contact me here

annvoorhis@yahoo.com

Made in the USA
Columbia, SC
06 May 2020